# How People Get Food

## How People Produce, Change, and Move Food

### DEVELOPED IN COOPERATION
### WITH
### THE CHILDREN'S MUSEUM OF INDIANAPOLIS
### INDIANAPOLIS, INDIANA

Copyright © 1993 by Scholastic Inc.        All rights reserved. Published by Scholastic Inc.        Printed in the U.S.A.

ISBN 0-590-26145-2

1 2 3 4 5 6 7 8 9 10        09        99 98 97 96 95 94 93 92

**TECHNOLOGY**

PEOPLE APPLY TOOLS, SKILLS, AND SCIENTIFIC KNOWLEDGE TO SOLVE
PROBLEMS AND EXTEND HUMAN CAPABILITIES.

# How People Get Food

People have invented ways to produce, process,
and distribute food.

Read-Aloud

How People
Get Food

**A**s the human population grows, more food must be
produced to feed the greater numbers of people.

Literature

**I**nventions that have solved food problems have caused new problems that people are working to solve.

THE MILK MAKERS

By Gail Gibbons

erature

**F**ood must be safely moved from places where it is produced to places where people buy it.

# What Do You Eat?

How many different kinds of food do you eat?
Does everybody eat the same kind of food?

## Sort some food.

**You need:**
Food packages
Magazines
Food coupons
Paper
Crayons or markers
Tape or glue

**❶** What foods don't have packages?
Find or draw pictures of them.

**❷** Sort packages, pictures, and
coupons into groups.

**❸** Use these groups to make a big
wall chart. What group is the biggest?
How many of your foods are made
from grains?

People eat lots of grains, such as wheat, rice, and corn. Farmers all over the world grow more than 1,000,000,000 tons of these grains each year.

THINK!
Why do people eat more grain than any other kind of food?

# Where Does Food Come From?

You saw all different kinds of food on your wall chart. All those foods come from different places. Where do the foods in pizza come from?

Almost all grains and vegetables come from large crop farms.

Some foods grow on trees in groves or orchards.

Ranchers and dairy farmers raise animals for meat and milk products.

Where else do people get food?

THINK!
Where does the pizza crust come from?

# How Do Farmers Farm?

You can use a shovel to dig up the soil for a home garden. But how would you get the soil ready to plant a big field of wheat?

Plows turn over the soil.

Seeders plant the seeds.

Many farm machines are pulled by tractors.

Cultivators pull the weeds.

A combine picks the crop.

THINK!
Why can farmers produce more food with machines than without them?

# What Must Farmers Plan For?

Besides planting, what else must farmers do to grow healthy crops?

If too little rain falls, the crops may die. Some farmers irrigate, or bring water from wells or reservoirs to their fields.

To keep insects from destroying their crops, many farmers spray chemicals on their fields or buy helpful insects to eat the harmful ones.

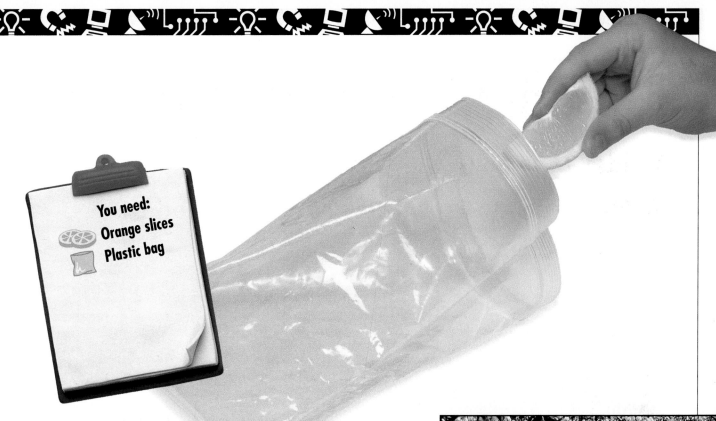

You need:
Orange slices
Plastic bag

# Freeze fruit.

❶ Look closely at your orange slice. What do you see? Put your slice in the plastic bag. Put the bag in the freezer. Wait one hour.

❷ Take the orange out of the freezer. What does it look like? Wait one hour. Now what do you see?

What might farmers do when it gets too cold for their crops?

THINK!
What problems could there be from chemicals that kill insects?

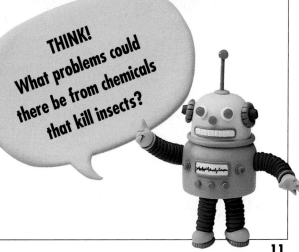

# Do Farmers Always Need Soil?

Certain food crops, like wheat, need a lot of land and soil to grow. How can some food be grown without soil?

You need:
Growing solution
Cup with lid
Screen
Cheesecloth
Alfalfa seeds
Water

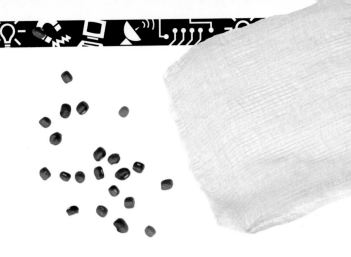

# Grow a water crop.

**1** Put the growing solution in the cup. Float the screen in the solution, and lay the cheesecloth on top of it.

**2** Place a seed over each screen hole. Put your cup in a warm sunny place.

**3** Check your cup every day. Add water to keep the same level. ✏️

THINK!
How does growing food in water help people?

Lettuce and some other foods can be grown in water when you add the minerals found in good soil. This kind of farming is called hydroponics.

# How Do People Farm the Waters?

Not all your food comes from the land. Fish and other water animals can be raised in underwater farms. What do you think they would need to grow?

You need:
Bottle
Salt water
Brine shrimp eggs
Spoon
Food

## Farm some shrimp.

❶ Fill the bottle with the salt water. Add a spoonful of shrimp eggs and stir gently.

❷ Observe the eggs several times a day. What happens?

❸ After two days, add a pinch of food. Do this every day.

Some of the shrimp that people eat is grown by farmers. Farmers collect shrimp eggs and hatch them in seawater ponds.

Trout need cold water. They're raised in mountain ponds where there's plenty of pure, cold water.

THINK! How else do people get fish from the water?

# How Do People Fish?

Most of the fish you eat aren't farmed. They are caught in oceans, rivers, or lakes. How do people get this food from the water?

Big fishing boats use sonar to find schools of fish. Then they drag huge nets through the water to catch the fish.

**You need:**
Newspapers
Pan or bowl
Water
Plastic bag
String
Paper fish

# Go fish.

**1** Make a net. Poke lots of holes in a bag, and attach string at each side.

**2** Put paper fish in a pan of water. Dip the bag at one end of the pan. Now try to catch fish of just one color. What happens?

**THINK!**
How are big fishing boat nets like your net?

# What Makes Good Food Go Bad?

What happens when you leave fish or milk out on the kitchen counter too long?

You need:
Bread
Plastic bag
Paper
Water

## Bag it.

❶ Put one piece of bread in a plastic bag and one piece on paper. Leave them out for a few hours. What happens?

❷ Put water on both pieces of bread. Put the first piece back in its bag. Leave both pieces in a warm place. Check every day and see what happens.

If food is not carefully handled, preserved, packaged, or stored, it can go bad before you use it.

THINK!
What could happen if you eat food that has spoiled?

# How Can You Preserve Food?

People have learned how to preserve food. Long ago they salted and smoked fish and meat. How did they save plant foods?

You need:
Apples
String
Tape

# Preserve some fruit.

**1** String your apple slices together, and hang them in a sunny place.

**2** Look at the slices every day. How are they changing? Taste one. How does it taste?

THINK!
What foods besides apples can easily be dried?

# How Can You Keep Food Cold?

Cold slows down the spoiling of food.
If you want to keep something cool,
you have to keep heat away from it.

You need:
Box
Paper
Plastic
Aluminum foil
Ice cubes

# Keep it cool.

❶ Use your materials to design an ice keeper.

❷ Put an ice cube on the table and one in your ice keeper. Which one lasts longer? Why? What materials work best?

How is your ice keeper like a refrigerator? How is it different?

THINK!
Why do people store food in the freezer?

# Why Are Some Foods Packaged?

Factories make and preserve many foods and put them in packages. Why are there so many kinds of packages?

You need:
Crackers
Plastic bag
Cup
Brown paper
String
Cloth
Wax paper
Small boxes

# Pack it up.

**1** Put a cracker in a plastic bag and carry it around for a day. What happens?

**2** Use your materials to design a safe package for the crackers.

**3** Now what happens when you carry your package around for a day?

What foods grow their own packages?

THINK!
Why is it bad for foods to get too much packaging?

25

# How Does Food Get to Your Town?

You know that some foods are packaged in factories. Others go straight from farms and fishing boats to food markets. How do they all get to where you live?

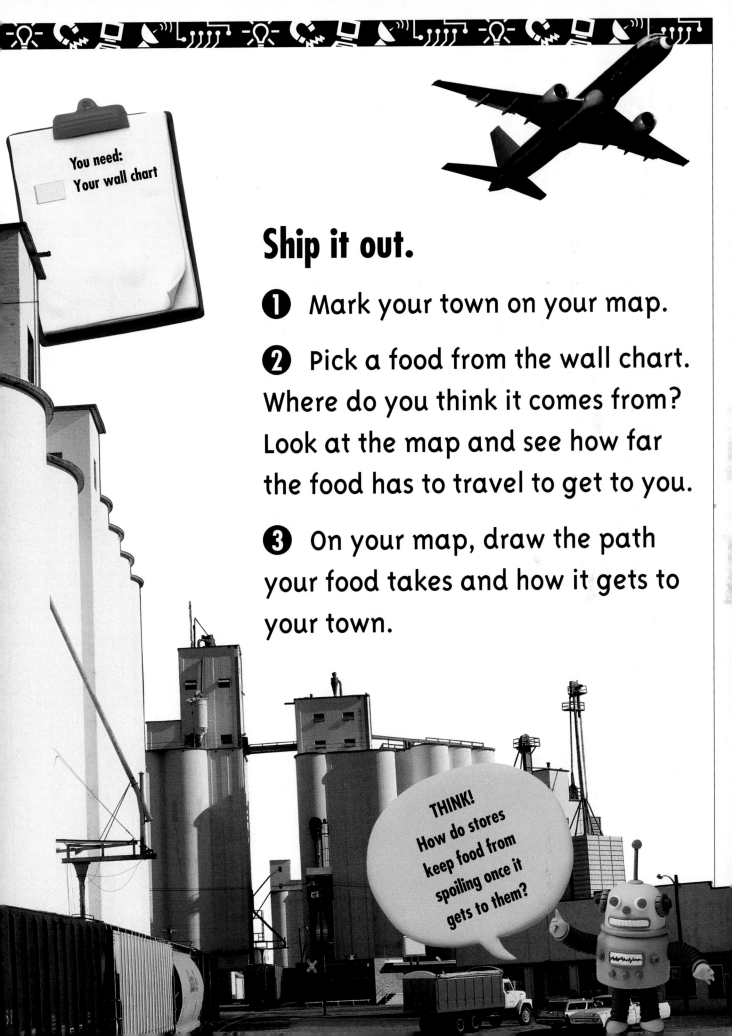

You need:
Your wall chart

## Ship it out.

**1** Mark your town on your map.

**2** Pick a food from the wall chart. Where do you think it comes from? Look at the map and see how far the food has to travel to get to you.

**3** On your map, draw the path your food takes and how it gets to your town.

THINK!
How do stores keep food from spoiling once it gets to them?

# How Is Food Distributed?

Food doesn't always come straight to your store. Some foods go to a food center first. These centers then sell the food to grocery stores, hospitals, schools, or restaurants.

FRUIT AND VEGETABLE DISTRIBUTION CENTER

VEGETABLES

FRUIT

RESTAURANT
Good Family Cooking

THINK!
Which of these places do you get most of your food from?

# What's the Story of Your Favorite Food?

What's your favorite food? What is it made from?
How is it grown? How does it get to you?

You need:
Construction paper
Markers or
crayons
Yarn

# Cook Up a Food Story.

**1** Tell the story of your favorite food by writing one sentence each on six pieces of paper. Add a picture to each page.

**2** Hold all your pages together and punch holes on the side. Now tie your food story together with yarn.

**Chemicals:** Everything is a chemical or a mixture of chemicals. Farmers use chemicals made by people to add minerals to the soil or kill harmful insects.

**Crops:** Crops are plants that are grown on farms for food.

**Distribute:** To distribute something is to give out portions of it to many places or people.

**Grain:** A grain is the seed of a grass plant. Wheat, rice, corn, oats, and barley are some grains.

**Hydroponics:** Hydroponic farming is a way to grow crops in water instead of soil.

**Irrigate:** To irrigate is to bring water to dry land through canals or sprinklers. Farmers get the water from reservoirs or by digging wells.